# WILD BIRDS OF PREY!

# EAGLES
# AND OSPREY

## By Deborah Kops

BLACKBIRCH PRESS, INC.
WOODBRIDGE, CONNECTICUT

Published by Blackbirch Press, Inc.
260 Amity Road
Woodbridge, CT 06525

**Email:** staff@blackbirch.com
**Web site:** www.blackbirch.com

©2000 by Blackbirch Press, Inc.

Dedication
For John

—DK

Printed in the United States

10 9 8 7 6 5 4 3 2

**Photo Credits:** Cover: ©Harold Wilson/Cornell Ornithology; page 4: ©D. Robert Franz/Cornell Ornithology; pages 5, 18: ©Isidor Jeklin/Cornell Ornithology; pages 6, 7, 9-11, 15: ©Corel Corporation; page 8: ©James Weaver/Cornell Ornithology; page 12: ©Patrick Grace/Photo Researchers; pages 13, 14, 16, 21 (bottom), 22: ©PhotoDisc; page 17: ©Fritz Polking/Peter Arnold; page 19: ©O.S. Pettingill/Cornell Ornithology; page 20: ©Tom & Pat Leeson; page 21 (top): ©Rick Kline/Cornell Ornithology.

**Library of Congress Cataloging-in-Publication Data**
Kops, Deborah.
Eagles and osprey / by Deborah Kops:
    p.   cm. — (Wild birds of prey)
   Includes bibliographical references.
   Summary: Discusses two raptors, the eagle and the osprey, including their physical characteristics, hunting and feeding habits, reproduction, and relationship with humans.
   ISBN 1-56711-270-6
   1. Eagles—Juvenile literature. 2. Osprey—Juvenile literature. [1. Eagles. 2. Osprey.] I. Title II. Series.
QL696.F32K68   2000
598.9'42—dc21
                                          99-36998
                                          CIP

# Contents

# Introduction

If you live by the ocean, you may have seen an osprey cruising over the water in search of a flounder. With its M-shaped wings, its profile against the sky looks like a giant sea gull. Or maybe you spent some time out West and were lucky enough to spot a golden eagle soaring high above a dry valley filled with sagebrush.

Eagles and osprey are birds of prey, which are also called raptors. Other raptors include hawks, falcons, vultures, and owls.

Bald eagles are found only in North America.

Like most birds, raptors eat other animals. They are among the best hunters in the bird world. Whether it's an 8-inch- (20-centimeter) tall saw-whet owl or a bald eagle about 4 times its size, the body of a raptor is designed for hunting. Raptors have long, curved claws—called talons—which they use for grabbing and killing their prey. They also have sharp, hooked beaks to help them tear at the animal they have caught.

Osprey live in more places than any other raptor.

Osprey are found in more places in the world than any other bird of prey. Eagles are found on every continent except Antarctica. There are 59 species, or kinds, of eagles, but only 1 kind of osprey. The 2 species of eagle common in North America are golden eagles and bald eagles.

# Members of the Family

A bald eagle isn't really bald. Its name comes from an old English word that means "white," the color of the feathers on its head. This large bird is a majestic flier. Sometimes it travels slowly, using powerful wing beats. Other times it soars through the air in the company of other eagles.

### Bald Eagles

Bald eagles are found only in North America. Because they like to eat fish, they usually live near an ocean, river, or lake. In spring and summer, many bald eagles live in Canada and in northern parts of the United States, especially along the coast of Alaska.

**Left:** Bald eagles were named for the white feathers on their heads.
**Opposite:** Eagles beat their wings in powerful thrusts or extend them straight out to soar.

These coastal areas are eagle breeding grounds, where they nest and raise their young. Bald eagles that live on a coast may stay there all year. Others migrate south in fall and spend the winter in areas that have warmer water temperatures. One popular destination is the Mississippi River. There, they can find a good supply of fish.

### Golden Eagle

Golden eagles live in wide open spaces in Europe, Asia, and North America. This raptor is named for the patches of gold-colored feathers on its neck. The rest of the bird's feathers are mostly brown. They cover the eagle's body and legs, all the way down to its feet.

In the United States, golden eagles live in the tall-grass prairies, pastureland, and deserts of the West year-round. In Canada, however, some goldens nest and raise their young on the treeless tundra in the far north. Then they fly south in fall. Goldens are excellent hunters as well as fliers.

In North America, golden eagles live in tall-grass prairies, pastures, deserts, and even on tundra in Canada.

## Osprey

Brown-and-white osprey are about two-thirds of the size of bald eagles.

In North America, osprey share their spring and summer habitats—the Great Lakes region and along the Atlantic coast—with bald eagles. In fall, they migrate much farther than balds do. Osprey will travel as far south as Central and South America and the Caribbean Sea.

Osprey are commonly found near water.

## Choosing a National Symbol

In 1782, when the United States was still a new nation, Thomas Jefferson and John Adams chose a bald eagle to appear on the national seal. They believed the bald eagle is a sign of strength and courage. They also liked that it lived only in North America. Benjamin Franklin disagreed with their choice. He was bothered by the fact that bald eagles sometimes steal fish from osprey. "He is a bird of bad moral character," Franklin protested. "[The bald eagle] does not get his living honestly." Franklin was proposing that the turkey become the national bird. Adams and Jefferson won the argument. Today the bald eagle is on many official things, including the national seal, which is on the back of a one-dollar bill.

# Eagle and Osprey Bodies

Golden eagles, bald eagles, and osprey are among the largest raptors in North America. Goldens and balds are about the same size. Their enormous wingspans, measured from the tip of one wing to the tip of the other, range from 6 to 7.5 feet (1.8–2.3 meters). That's more than twice the length of

Raptors are excellent fliers because their wings are large and powerful and their bodies are light.

their bodies! Osprey have wingspans that commonly range between 5 and 5.5 feet (1.5–1.7 meters). They're about 2 feet (.6 meters) long from the tips of their beaks to the ends of their tails.

Eagles and osprey are great fliers for several reasons. In addition to having very large wings, these birds have light bodies. An average bald eagle weighs only 9 pounds (4 kilograms). That's about 2 pounds (1 kilogram) less than an average house cat.

An eagle's wide wings make it especially good at soaring.

Like most raptors, osprey and eagles occasionally soar through the air. An eagle's wide wings make it especially good at this kind of flight. When the sun warms the ground, a current of rising warm air—called a thermal—is sometimes created. When an eagle or osprey flies into the middle of a thermal, it stretches out its wings and rises with the air. In a big thermal, a soaring eagle can climb 3 miles (4.8 kilometers) high!

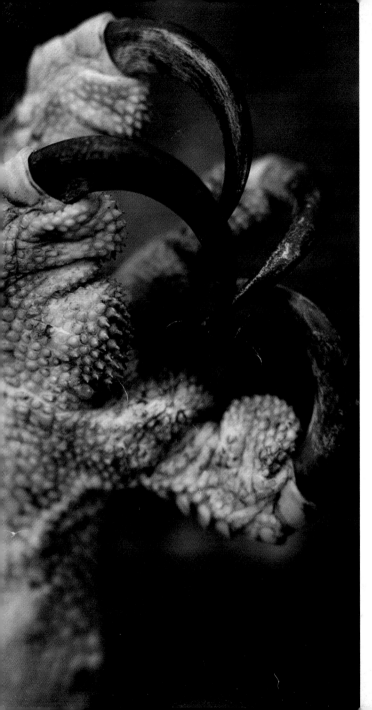

# Special Features

Raptors have strong feet and sharp talons. These features help the birds attack and transport prey. Large, powerful wings also provide excellent lifting ability. Golden eagles, for example, can carry prey as large as a young sheep! Bald eagles and osprey have bumps on their toes for gripping the slippery bodies of their favorite prey—fish.

Osprey feet have another helpful feature. Unlike most raptors, which have 3 toes facing front and 1 toe facing back, osprey have a "reversible" outer toe. This toe can swing around to the back of the foot, so that there are 2 toes facing back and 2 facing front. This helps an osprey hold onto a wriggling fish.

Birds of prey have sharp talons for gripping and ripping prey. **Opposite:** Large eyes, sharp beaks, and long talons make raptors excellent hunters.

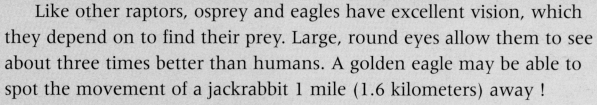

Like other raptors, osprey and eagles have excellent vision, which they depend on to find their prey. Large, round eyes allow them to see about three times better than humans. A golden eagle may be able to spot the movement of a jackrabbit 1 mile (1.6 kilometers) away !

Once it has caught and killed its prey with its talons, an osprey or eagle uses its hooked beak to tear at its meal. The beak is made out of bone and covered with keratin—the same material that makes up your fingernails.

# Hunting

Bald eagles and osprey have somewhat different styles of catching fish. An osprey soars hundreds of feet above the water. When it sees a fish, it tucks in its wings and dives, plunging down to the water. Just when you think it will enter head first, it adjusts its wingspan and catches with its feet.

Powerful vision allows bald eagles to wait high above and far away until they spot prey.

A bald eagle likes to hunt from a perch that has a good view of the water, such as a high tree branch. It waits patiently until it spots a fish. Then it flies feet first toward the water, stretching out its legs. The eagle swoops over the water and grasps the fish with its talons. Then it returns to its perch to enjoy its meal. Unlike an osprey, it has barely gotten wet. A bald eagle also has another way of getting its food—it steals prey from ducks, gulls, osprey, and other bald eagles. This kind of hunting is called piracy.

Golden eagles often soar over open country, diving suddenly to grab a startled jackrabbit or some other small animal. A golden can dive at a speed of over 100 miles (161 kilometers) an hour! Sometimes it hunts with its mate. If an animal gets away from the first bird, the second golden tries to grab it.

Bald eagles swoop down feet first and then lower their feet into the water to grab a fish.

# The Food Supply

Osprey are very good at catching fish, and are sometimes called fish hawks. They mostly hunt fish that they can easily carry from the water, such as

flounder or shad. Bald eagles prefer to eat salmon. In fall, thousands of balds gather along the Chilkat River in Alaska. They catch the salmon jumping out of the water and swimming upriver to spawn (lay eggs).

Eagles and osprey can't always find their prey of choice. Although golden eagles prefer to hunt smaller prey, they also eat much larger mammals, including foxes. When food is scarce, goldens have been known to kill young farm animals. Sometimes they eat gamebirds, snakes, and even large insects. Balds will eat ducks, turtles, and small mammals, such as rabbits.

Two bald eagles share their prey in the safety of their nest.

Osprey are especially good at catching fish and are sometimes called fish hawks.

All 3 birds will eat carrion (already-dead animals). Goldens and osprey do this only occasionally, when there is little else. Bald eagles aren't as fussy. In winter, they will even pick scraps from garbage dumps.

# Mating and Nesting

Eagles are known for their spectacular courtship displays. This is a type of behavior that all birds use to attract a mate for the breeding season. Birds do this even if they keep the same mate for life, as most eagles do.

Before pairing off, balds perform all kinds of acrobatics in the air, including cartwheeling. A pair will lock their talons together and spiral down thousands of feet before separating. Goldens like to circle high in the air and dive at each other. Osprey show interest by chasing each other.

Eagles pair off and often keep the same mates for life.

Once these raptors select their mates, they begin to work on their large nests (called aeries), to which they add every year. A famous bald eagle nest in Ohio weighed 2 tons when it finally broke the tree in which it rested! Eagle and osprey nests are usually high off the ground, and are often built from thick sticks and branches. Osprey will also use some human-made materials in their constructions, such as Styrofoam cups and fabric.

.After the nest is built, the female lays her eggs. Eagles lay 1 or 2 eggs, and osprey usually lay 3. The parents then take turns sitting on the eggs to keep them warm. This incubation process goes on for 35 to 45 days.

Eagles and osprey build large, heavy nests called aeries, high above the ground.

# Raising Young

Newly hatched eagle and osprey chicks are covered with down (soft, light-colored feathers). At first, they are quite helpless. Their parents tear up meat and feed it to them. One parent guards the young while the other one hunts. Osprey parents need to do a lot of fishing. Three young osprey eat 6 pounds (2.7 kilograms) of fish a day!

Baby eagles are covered in soft, light-colored feathers called down.
**Opposite:** Parents continue to care for their young and provide them with food for the first 6 months.
**Top:** A golden mother offers her chick some partially digested solid food.
**Bottom:** A bald eagle mother guards her young on the nest.

Within a few weeks, the flight feathers of young eagles and osprey begin to grow, and the down falls out. At this stage, young balds and goldens look very similar. A 6-month-old bald eagle (called an eaglet) has mostly brown feathers. Its head won't be completely white until it is about 4-and-a-half years old. By then, the eagle will have about 7,000 feathers!

When they are about 10 weeks old, the birds are ready to make their first attempts at flying. This is called fledging. Although it signals the end of the nesting period, parents continue to provide their young with some food and teach them to hunt. Golden eagle parents care for their young in this way for another 3 months.

Learning to hunt and survive on their own is difficult for young osprey and eagles—more than half do not survive to adulthood. The birds that do survive often live 20 or 30 years in the wild. In captivity (cared for by humans), they live almost twice as long.

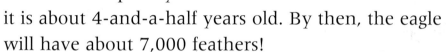

# Osprey, Eagles, and Humans

Humans have been the biggest threat to the survival of osprey and eagles. In recent years, strict protection laws have been passed to help these magnificent birds increase in number.

In the past, large numbers of golden eagles were killed by sheep ranchers who thought the eagles were preying on their lambs. But in 1962, it became illegal to kill these birds. Since then, the golden eagle population has remained at about 20,000 nesting pairs in North America.

In the 1950s and 1960s, Americans and Canadians began spraying farm crops and forests with a chemical called DDT. This chemical killed harmful insects. But it also polluted rivers, lakes, and oceans.

Because of human activities, bald eagles used to be endangered in the United States. With human help, their population has returned to a healthy level.

## Moving a Golden Eagle Family

Howard and Bonnie Postovit are professional movers—eagle movers, that is. These two scientists live in northeast Wyoming near the Powder River. This is golden eagle territory, and it is also where a lot of coal is mined.

When a mining company wants to dig for coal in a place where golden eagles are nesting, it hires Bonnie and Howard's company—Powder River Eagle Studies—to move the family so it will not be harmed. The relocation process takes many weeks. Howard and Bonnie choose a spot where the parents like to spend time, a safe distance from the new mine. Then they move the family in stages. They use a movable platform and a new nest, which Howard builds. One pair of eagles has been using Howard's nest for 19 years—with many additions of their own, of course.

Certain fish that lived in those waters became poisonous. When bald eagles and osprey ate those affected fish, they became poisoned, too. (Goldens were not affected). They didn't die, but the females laid eggs with very thin shells. When the parents tried to sit on the eggs to incubate them, the shells broke.

In the early 1970s, the United States and Canada passed laws that made it illegal to use DDT. At that time, there were only about 400 nesting pairs of bald eagles left in the lower 48 United States, which do not include Alaska. There are now about 5,500 pairs of bald eagles in the "lower 48," and about 14,000 pairs of osprey. That's a great comeback!

# Glossary

**breeding grounds**  The place where birds nest and raise their young.

**carrion**  The meat of a dead animal.

**distributed**  Spread out over a region.

**incubate**  To keep eggs warm until they hatch.

**soar**  To fly high in the air without much effort.

**species**  One of a group of animals (or plants) that are alike in some way. Members of the same species can have young together.

**tundra**  A cold area where there are no trees. Under the surface, the ground in this habitat is permanently frozen.

# For More Information

## Books

Kalman, Bobbie. *Raptors.* New York: Crabtree Publishing Company, 1998.

Parry-Jones, Jemima. *Amazing Birds of Prey.* New York: Alfred A. Knopf, 1992.

Patent, Dorothy Hinshaw. *Eagles of America.* New York: Holiday House, 1995.

## Web Site

*The Eagle's Nest*

Information and photographs of different eagle species—www.eaglesnest.com/eagles.html

# Index